Dedicated to those who have helped me soar. Especially my husband, Chris, and our three little chickens: Blake, Grant and Kate.

# design

## HER

JULIANNE TAYLOR

Printed in China

First Printing, 2015

ISBN 978-0-9963820-1-4

Fashion + Decor Publishing
info@fashiondecor.com

www.fashiondecor.com

INSPIRING ENTREPRENEURS SHAPING
TODAY'S HOME DÉCOR INDUSTRY

# design HER

## JULIANNE TAYLOR

Fashion + Decor Publishing

# Content

# Foreword

When we think of powerful women in the interiors and product design industry, Julianne of Taylor Burke Home always comes to mind. We first came across Taylor Burke Home at one of the July Atlanta trade show markets several years ago. It was love at first sight when her furniture caught our eye – fresh and young in design. We were immediately obsessed!

Julianne Taylor, "Mama" as we lovingly call her, is the epitome of a strong, determined businesswoman. Since our first trade show introduction, we have developed a deep-rooted friendship with Julianne. We knew we were meant to be lifelong friends after Julianne attended a dinner party at our home and screamed in joy when she saw a piece of art hanging in our stairwell. The piece had once belonged to her during her time in Shanghai and had made its way to our home via several other vendors.

When we heard that Julianne was writing this book, we thought it was a fabulous way to celebrate not only her talent and amazingly fast success but also other successful women in the design industry. We are extremely honored to be writing the foreword. What a talented group of women she profiles within these pages. This book is not only a great way to celebrate inspiring women in design, but it will also act as a resource for readers to gain knowledge around amazing products and talent. Cheers to *DesignHER!*

LANCE JACKSON & DAVID ECTON
Interior Designers
Parker Kennedy Living

# Introduction

## A NOTE FROM THE AUTHOR

The idea for *DesignHER* first came about in a similar manner as many other designers' first books. Industry colleagues started asking me when I might be "doing a book," as it is often expected at some point in your career. I'd shrug my shoulders and raise my eyebrows as if to say "me?" Writing a book seemed daunting to me at the time. I had too many balls in the air. I also wondered if an audience would truly be interested in my perspective. Around the same time, I started noticing a pattern. Through industry events and my work at trade shows in Atlanta, High Point, and Las Vegas, women in business seemed to gravitate toward me. They came to me for business insight, and I welcomed their questions and responded honestly. It's just who I am. I found myself agreeing to set up mentoring calls with other women in the industry and having business strategy discussions over drinks at industry events. I began to question why there weren't more female mentors in the home décor industry. This business seemed like a big ole boys club. I wondered if I, as one individual, could make a difference. What could I contribute that might pave the way for other female entrepreneurs?

Though I had no energy to write a book about myself, I found an enormous amount of passion for writing a book to teach, share, and inspire rising entrepreneurs. I love making pretty things, but I want my legacy to be more than that. As a woman of deep faith, I want to *DO* something. I want to make a difference. I want to inspire my children to reach their full potential and teach them that dreams really can come true with hard work.

John F. Kennedy once said, "a rising tide lifts all boats." This poignant thought hits me right at the core. As we raise each other up, we can all be more successful. I've also heard the saying many times, "if women weren't so focused on tearing each other down, we could rule the world." Many ladies reading this will agree that we have been on the receiving end of some mean girl action at some point in our personal or professional lives. We have created such an environment of competition, that many of us avoid connecting with other women to protect ourselves. Not only is the experience unpleasant, it's unnecessary. *DesignHER* is my way of turning the tables and lifting the tide.

I am thrilled to present you with the stories of some truly inspiring women. I hope you enjoy reading them as much as I've enjoyed getting to know the women featured. By celebrating the success of each individual in this book, we set the stage for continued support, collaboration, and connection that has the power to elevate us all.

XO,
Julianne

*Patrick Family,*

## Julianne Taylor

TAYLOR BURKE HOME

*Remember to always Dream Big! Xo,*

*Julianne*

My story began overseas as I followed my husband's corporate career all over the world. Having a degree in Interior Design and a masters in Human Resources, I enjoyed careers in both fields before getting married and moving abroad. I left a successful career in human resources just days before a wedding and a move to Australia.  Now as the trailing spouse living overseas, I had to figure out what my next move would be.  I had always worked.  What was I supposed to do now? I didn't even have a work visa!  I found myself restless and wondering what my new identity would be.

New friends soon found out that I had formal training and experience in interior design and jumped at the chance to get advice. I realized quickly that I had a niche market as a westerner, living abroad, practicing interior design. As we moved from Melbourne to Barcelona, Shanghai, and eventually Seoul, I carved out a nice little home based interior design business working with expats all over the world. As the economic bubble was bursting in the U.S. in 2007/2008, I enjoyed a captive audience of expat wives with access to extra disposable income. My time in Shanghai was a unique experience as an Interior Designer as I had factories at my fingertips willing to make anything for me with a simple photo as inspiration. Making custom furniture for clients was inspiring and FUN. I was bitten hard by the furniture design bug and began to feel that my years abroad gave me a unique perspective on product development.

I officially launched Taylor Burke Home in January 2012 on our dining room table in Seoul, Korea. Now a family of five, the pregnancy years were just in my rear view mirror. I was itching to do something more and stretch my talents into product development. We took part of our savings that year as the seed money to start my company. I remember having feelings of fear, that I might lose it all and we would never get that money back. My husband, Chris, reassured me, "I would rather you try and lose it all than to never try at all." He has been my biggest supporter from the very start and has always believed in me.

I connected with the S.C.O.R.E. Charlotte chapter and found a wonderful small business mentor. He reviewed my business plan and gave me great advice on start-up pitfalls.

We fumbled around with names such as Julianne Taylor Collection and Julianne Taylor Home. We finally settled on the name Taylor Burke Home to honor my close relationship with my sister, Lauren Burke. With the goal to show my first collection in July 2012 at AmericasMart in Atlanta, I loaded up a container full of product I had manufactured in Shanghai and shipped it to the U.S. just in time for the show. I laugh now thinking about our first booth on the seventh floor of building one. We were sandwiched between temporary vendors selling bear rugs and candles! The scent from the candles was so strong that I had a severe headache the entire market. I remember thinking, "Good grief! This is not as glamorous as I thought it was going to be!" My sister was a real trooper in getting the company off the ground. She helped in the beginning when I could not afford to hire anyone, and worked 14-hour days during the first few trade shows to help me sell product. The naiveté of those times brings a smile now to both of our faces.

After our very first show in Atlanta, we quickly moved to showing in High Design and HD-Home at Americasmart, in High Point Market, and we've dabbled a bit in the Las Vegas show. In October 2015 we opened a permanent showroom in the Atlanta Decorative Arts Center (ADAC) to showcase our products

along with other premium brands. Moving to a permanent space in Atlanta is key to our long-term growth strategy. Not to mention the many times I've been up on a ladder hanging lights in the showroom after pulling an all-nighter and thinking, "I'm getting too old for this." Ha! We are now rethinking the way that we go to market to align with customer buying patterns and to ensure balance in my personal life. Both are essential to our growth plan moving forward.

I learned many lessons along the way in starting my own company. My husband, Chris, calls me "weeble wobble". He says, "People or situations may get you down, but you get right back up!" This was never more evident in a situation that happened early on that could have completely derailed the launch of Taylor Burke Home. The container I loaded and shipped to the U.S. from Shanghai for my first collection was shipped by a fraudulent freight forwarder in Shanghai. I was living in Seoul, and we later found out the freight forwarding company in Shanghai shipped my container, but told me it was being held by Chinese customs. I needed to pay US $10,000 in order to get customs to release my container. I was familiar with this tactic in China, as I had lived there prior to our relocation to Seoul. I knew immediately that the company was trying to extort money from me. I called everyone I knew that might be able to help. In the end, after $200 in consulting fees, I got the container released to me from right under his nose. As my close friends will tell you, "Good luck trying to pull one over on Mama!."

As my business has grown, each step presents a new set of challenges and concerns to make sure we are growing in the right way. Hands down one of the best decisions I've made is to hire a Head of Business Development. She is truly my right-hand person. As we review and consider product development, licensing deals, and creative projects, she ensures that they align with our branding strategy. I fully believe that you always need a person that pushes back and has healthy debate with you about the business. A "yes ma'am" individual is not going to take your business to the next level.

I believe our success has been due to our downright hard work and our keen ability to develop strong relationships. I saw early on that I could create beautiful showrooms by partnering with other design driven companies. Financially it made sense, and the shopping experience for our buyers is better. By cross-merchandising our showrooms, it shows our buyers how to style different products and brands together. It's more interesting! I remember other company owners would come by during market and ask, "how in the world did you pull that off working with other vendors?!" Let's face it; if you own your own company, you've got an ego. *And* some egos are the size of Mount Rushmore in this business, people! I fully believe that if you can set your ego and controlling tendencies aside, you can work with multiple brands to create a beautiful showroom. We have had wonderful experiences with Cotton + Quill, Dunes & Duchess, Addison Weeks, Mitchell Black, Lacefield and Times Two Design. We are always looking for collaborative vendor partners that are a good match in both aesthetic and target customer.

What's on the horizon for us? In addition to our foray into permanent showrooms, we are incredibly passionate about programs that support female entrepreneurs and developing tools to support the creative community as a whole. We now have a consulting component of our business that offers various branding and business strategy workshops for small and large companies in the creative arena. I am also extremely passionate about product development and plan to seek every growth opportunity available in this area.

Thinking of starting your own business? Formalize a good business plan and thoroughly research your market. Talk to everyone you can to gain information about your industry. In the end, at some point you just have to go for it! It will be the hardest you have ever worked, but you will be fulfilled beyond your wildest imagination.

www.taylorburkehome.com

# Meg Braff

MEG BRAFF DESIGNS, LLC

I can recall seeing Meg Braff published in every magazine under the sun for as long as I can remember. Then the gorgeous green trellis wallpaper installed in the Farmington, Connecticut retail store, Vivid Hue Home, alerted me to the true extent of her talents. A beautiful photo of our Kings Grant Chairs in ebony with zebra print cowhide placed in front of Braff's wallpaper was Instagrammed across the universe. It had me gasping. I soon had the pleasure of meeting Braff at High Point Market and was struck by the down to earth and humble personality of this big city designer.

Braff has operated an award-winning interior design firm, Meg Braff Interiors, since 1994. In 2011 she launched her wallpaper collection company, Meg Braff Designs, LLC, and opened an antique and design retail store in Locust Valley, New York. Braff now says these are hands down the best two moves she has made for her brand. Braff's offerings now include a small fabric line and she hopes to venture into furniture categories in the future.

One of Braff's biggest challenges in product development has been designing lines that can withstand the test of time. Braff says, "My favorite patterns and colors change constantly, and it was a bit scary at first to create products that would be timeless." There have been a few times that Braff didn't go with her gut on a color. She says, "When it was all said and done, I wished that I had. When you look at the bigger picture, a different color could have had a completely different impact on the collection as a whole."

As Braff's business grows, she admits to struggling with keeping up with inquiries and orders. Braff says, "It's not as simple as it looks believe it or not. We are still a relatively small shop with a very broad reach. It is a challenge to get through every day." Braff's keys to success have been hard work and her love for design. Braff says, "I try to take every opportunity and put my all into it. A positive attitude has always been my best asset."

Thinking of starting your own company? Braff's advice is to, "Never give up! The second you doubt yourself you will be that much closer to failure."

www.megbraffdesigns.com

# Jill Sorensen

JILL SORENSEN

I stumbled upon Jill Sorensen on Instagram and quickly fell in love with her colorful and graphic bedding. Formerly a model, Sorensen fell into interior design after working with a designer on her own home. After endless requests to design homes, coupled with her frustration and difficulty in finding affordable, good designs and home furnishings, Jill founded her own interior design firm.

In 2009 Sorensen developed an idea to offer free space planning and online room design, in addition to design-driven home furnishings in an e-commerce setting. Sorensen created her website platform with a desire to help a large audience of people improve their surroundings at an inexpensive price point. Sorensen states, "Helping people help themselves really inspires me."

Sorensen had no idea how well her idea would take off. She quickly went from a small boutique design firm doing high-end homes to a successful online furnishings store with a design blog offering more affordable options. As her business expanded, Sorensen was challenged with finding bedding and rugs that suited her aesthetic. As a result, Sorensen designed her own collections and she soon found that these were the products selling the most in her online store. Sorensen was bitten by the product development bug!

One of the biggest obstacles Sorensen has faced is learning to succeed at marketing her products and services. "When you start a company, people mistakenly think it's all about designing. The truth is, 90 percent of your job is about marketing." As her business has evolved, Sorensen has rebranded her company three times, which has been a challenge for marketing her brand. "I had too many names. My design firm was called Marmalade Interiors, my online store and blog was called Live Like You, and my line of products was called Jill Sorensen. Very confusing and terrible for marketing purposes!" Sorensen streamlined her concepts and put it all under one name, Jill Sorensen, Inc. "In a way, a new name is like starting over, so it's best to figure out your branding up front."

Sorensen has learned to spend time on work that aligns with the big picture and goals for her company. She knows that it's easy to get sidetracked taking on jobs that might not align with the company vision. "There are only so many hours in the day; sometimes you need to learn to say no. You can't do everything well, so you have to choose the right projects to focus on," says Sorensen.

Sorensen's advice to young entrepreneurs: "Find something you love so much that you would do it for free. You will never work a day in your life. Be prepared to work longer and harder than everybody else. When you have your own business, you get what you put into it. Running your own company is 10 percent inspiration and 90 percent perspiration."

www.jillsorensen.com

# Ashley Childers

EMPORIUM HOME

I was drawn into the Emporium Home Showroom the first time I laid eyes on those gorgeous agate wall sconces that are the signature of Ashley Childers' style. As the head creative for the fast growing and popular Emporium Home, Childers started the company in 2012 after she had a difficult time finding lighting for her own home. Her brand creates lighting and furniture designs that mix natural stones with artisan metals and handcrafted quality. The designs that she produces are ones she loves and would want in her own home. As result, Emporium Home has a brand aesthetic that is distinctively unique.

The key to her success has been her ability to stay authentic. From the very beginning, she has personally designed every single piece in the Emporium Home collection. Some eyebrows were raised when she initially launched the company after a 13-year career as a dancer and choreographer. When you meet her, you have no doubt that those big beautiful eyes and gorgeous flowing hair once danced across a stage! Without any previous background in the home furnishings industry, learning the ins and outs of the industry has been integral to her success. "It's so glamorous to think about designing beautiful products. The reality is that we manage day to day production, fulfillment, logistics, quality control, marketing, customer service, schedules, and a thousand other things every day."

Childers will tell you that one of her biggest challenges in running her business is growing too fast. "We were so blessed to get some really great exposure early on and grew much faster than we ever expected. It was amazing that my designs were resonating with people, but we played catch up for awhile!"

One of the biggest lessons she has learned along the way is that you can't take everyone and everything at face value. "I tend to hand my trust out like candy-- flash me a smile and give me a strong handshake, and I am going to believe you are going to do what you say you will do. This has come back to bite me a few times in business."

Childers' advice to budding entrepreneurs is to, "Do your research, and work hard. Ask questions, and listen to the answers. Don't let setbacks be setbacks. Learn from them and move on. Be authentic, and embrace creativity. You should love every minute!"

www.emporiumhome.com

# Dana Gibson

## DANA GIBSON DESIGN

Dana Gibson and I first met on Instagram. We shared a mutual respect for each other's work and often commented back and forth. I was first exposed to her work when our chair was styled with her leopard print pillow for a photo shoot. I thought, "Who is this talented person?" As I soon discovered, Dana Gibson Inc. offers beautifully detailed hand-painted tole lamps, trays and small furnishings along with her signature textiles. She also has strong licensing partnerships with Stroheim, The MT Company, Soicher Marin and Hamilton Beach. Her inspiring story starts at a luxury department store in New York City.

Back in the early 1990s, Gibson was shopping at Henri Bendel in New York City and noticed brightly colored platters high on a shelf. As Gibson says, "I thought to myself, someone is having a blast making beautiful home accessories. I'd like to do that!" At the time Gibson was teaching in Baton Rouge, Louisiana, utilizing her master's degree in writing from the University of Virginia. She adored teaching, but she knew that occupation would not sustain her creative spirit. In the summers she took ceramics classes at the local university. She became lost in making three-foot high planters adorned with vines, fruits and intricate flowery details. She showed some early, rough work to an aunt who had a gift store, but as Gibson says, "She didn't bite." "My plates were wobbly and uneven. The glazes

were less than artfully applied!" She realized she needed to make something less unique and with a broader appeal for the home decor market. The first items she sold were charming flower vases with birds, poppies, pansies and bees that were crafted in the tradition of fine, European porcelains. She soon progressed to larger vases, bowls and tureens, and made her first big sale to Henri Bendel. Saks and Niemans soon followed and were customers for years.

Gibson's business grew, and she soon found herself surrounded by a staff of twelve before moving production to India in 2002. People advised her not to send manufacturing overseas, but Gibson says "The decision was a good one and it saved my company." Hard work has been essential to growing and building her business. As Gibson tells me, "Don't get into this line of work for the financial reward. You have to love doing it. I have unloaded containers when I had a skeleton staff, and I've gone to work at 4:00am as it was the only way to squeeze in some creative time." Gibson feels strongly about listening to her customers and says she has gotten some of her best ideas from them. However, she says, " I have also gotten some less-than-thoughtful advice, and I have learned to filter those ideas! You can read every manual out there and consult every expert, but what you have created -- your business -- is unique. Choosing the best advice for you and your situation is key." She also believes that keeping an ear out for trends and market movement has been important to the success of her business.

Gibson says that keeping track of inventory has been one of her biggest challenges as her business has grown over the years. She has figured out along the way the importance of delegating to her fully capable assistants who manage different parts of the business. Gibson also points out that showing customers the designer behind the brand made her a bit uncomfortable in the beginning. "I kind of wanted to remain invisible and let my work speak for itself". However, Gibson now sees the value of personal appearances and understands that this interaction is key to growing her business and providing her customers with products they want and need.

Gibson is currently working on another collection of fabric, trim, and wallpaper for Stroheim, and is licensing her designs for furniture and art. When she was around the age of ten, Gibson thought owning a fabric store with exotic textiles and embellishments would be her ideal job. As she says, "having a part in creating beautiful textiles is a dream come true." Her advice? "Choose a career in something you love and a believe in.  Then find a way to set yourself apart from others."

www.danagibsondesign.com

# Emily McCarthy

## EMILY MCCARTHY LLC

I connected with Emily McCarthy through some branding work she did for Parker Kennedy Living. Upon our first meeting, McCarthy oozed style. She was so well put together with her colorful pout and tortoise glasses. Her office space mimicked her personal style. We were immediate friends with a shared fondness for the other's creativity. Our meeting cooked up a fun licensing deal to develop entertainment essentials in McCarthy's signature look. Her Emily McCarthy for Taylor Burke Home bar cart and counter stools came out in early 2015. The design community was abuzz with delight.

McCarthy spent ten years in corporate retail, product development, and wholesale before setting out on her own. She knew it was time to follow her own design inspirations. McCarthy says, "With the support of my husband, I took the plunge and never looked back!" Founded in 2009, McCarthy's company initially focused on stationery and invitations. Through the years, the company has evolved into all facets of entertaining and style. "I found that not only did clients want the perfect invitation, they also wanted to know my opinion on what to wear and how to decorate. They wanted to know how to bring their own signature style to the event."

McCarthy admits that resources and manufacturing are always challenges for her. She says, "I often have big ideas for products and designs, but no direction on how to actually fabricate them." Despite tough manufacturing obstacles that many entrepreneurs face, McCarthy has partnered with companies like Cotton + Quill and ourselves to bring her home decor and textile designs to life. The spotted cheetah print fabric McCarthy created with Cotton + Quill was tweeted to the world earlier this year when it exploded onto the design scene. McCarthy credits social media as a great tool for getting the word out about her products and services.

Adding baby Lillian to her existing family of three in the summer of 2015 has created new challenges for this working mom. McCarthy's biggest challenge is carving out enough time to balance work and home. McCarthy says, "with a growing family, it's important to find time for everyone equally. My mind is always thinking of new designs and products. I try to jot down drawings right away." McCarthy knows that when she can find the right moment in her schedule for focused design time, she can take her drawings to further develop ideas on her computer.

McCarthy has learned along the way the importance of establishing a mutual understanding of time and financial investment before moving forward with her clients. She prefers to have a formal business agreement in place before doing any design work or sharing of ideas. "I find that unless a client is financially invested in your time, they don't take you seriously and will easily take your ideas elsewhere for a cheaper price."

McCarthy has clearly been bitten by the product development bug. Her future plans include expanding her licensed products to include more furniture, fabric and wall coverings. She would also enjoy developing apparel and accessories products that bring a little mid-century style into modern day fashion with her signature colors and fabrics. Watch out, world!

Thinking of starting your own company? McCarthy's advice is to "First work for someone else before starting your own business. You will learn so many valuable lessons and skills that school doesn't teach you."

www.emilymccarthy.com

# Anna Brockway

CHAIRISH

If you're looking for vintage or pre-owned decor and furniture, you've certainly come across the huge online curated marketplace known as Chairish. We at Taylor Burke Home have utilized Chairish to sell market samples, and many of our colleagues in the industry have had continued success as Chairish vendors. The initial spark for the idea of Chairish came when Brockway and her husband, Gregg, were moving houses. An entrepreneurial husband and his design-loving wife faced what seemed like a simple problem: How does one sell high quality furnishings that simply do not fit into their new home?

The Brockways soon found that many others shared this same problem. Job changes, moves, renovations, and style changes often led to an array of furniture and home decor that was perfectly usable but no longer suited a certain space. On the flip side, Anna Brockway found the process of finding just the right pieces for her new home time consuming. Figuring out transportation and delivery was a nightmare. With the goal of having a one-stop, full-service, curated destination for the best pre-owned and vintage furnishings, the Brockways assembled a group of co-founders to officially launch Chairish in 2013.

DAVID
HALBERSTAM          THE BEST AND
                    THE BRIGHTEST
                    FOREWORD BY SENATOR JOHN McCAIN

ALBERTO GIACOMETTI
DIEGO GIACOMETTI                           ASSOULINE
                                           ASSOULINE
DWELLINGS               Sills · Huniford

As Chief Curator, Anna Brockway ensures that their inventory is "fabulously stylish" by requiring that all 60,000+ items be pre-approved by her team. Brockway says their biggest obstacle in entering the market was awareness. "The decor and design industry is chocked full of interesting businesses and dazzling personalities. Making Chairish essential and unforgettable was our first challenge and is what we continue to focus on."

Chairish has been on a fast trajectory since their launch. Brockway and her team are challenged with maintaining the company's position as leading the vintage marketplace. "It's a bit like standing in the middle of a seesaw with the need to offer a hearty supply of inventory on one side and the need for shopper demand on the other. Keeping the balance between the two is our ongoing business objective." While a tough challenge to constantly stay in front of, it helps that Brockway is super passionate about her business. She confesses to being a compulsive re-decorator. "I love buying vintage pieces because of their killer style, immediate availability (no lead times), and fantastic prices."

Brockway credits her mother as an early influencer in her career. After 15 years as a stay at home mom, Brockway's mom went to law school and became a well-respected District Attorney. Similarly, Brockway says, "after being the Vice President of Worldwide Marketing at Levi Strauss, I took 10 years off to start a family. I founded Chairish as a 42-year-old mother of four. My mom showed me to go after what you want when you want it.

Brockway's advice for starting your own company: "If you wait for the right time or perfect plan, you'll never get started -- just get going! She also offers her favorite Reid Hoffman quote, "If you aren't embarrassed by the first version of your product, you launched too late."

www.chairish.com

# Katie Kime

KATIE KIME

The Katie Kime website is full of brightly colored upholstery, textiles, and even shift dresses that would tempt the most die-hard neutral lover. And let's talk about that banana leaf maxi skirt! Ummm...yes, please! This Austin-based superstar of all things home started at an early age. Kime remembers her favorite afterschool activity at the young age of seven was making clay pots at the school where her mom worked. Her love of creativity continued throughout her college years, and Kime soon found herself surrounded by her weekend creations. During her senior year at Duke University, Kime's friend hosted a trunk show for her. Kime says, "It was a collection of all one-of-a-kind items I had made -- a revamped dresser from the thrift store, handmade stationery, some paintings, etcetera. When I saw multiple product categories that I had made all in one place, the idea for what I'm currently doing came to life."

Kime spent the first five years after college apprenticing under various industries with the goal of one day building her own lifestyle brand. Kime says, "I learned about upholstery, interior design, sewing, acrylic manufacturing and product photography. Armed with the knowledge on all of these facets of the industry, I launched katiekime.com in 2013."

In the beginning, Kime recalls being told that she was too young to start her own company, but as she says, "Resilience has been the key to my success." Everyday brings a new challenge to Kime. She has been knocked down more than

a few times only to get back up. She says, "Designing and manufacturing multiple product lines across multiple states and countries means a lot of moving parts."

Financing, managing people, and mastering customer service have been challenges as Kime's business has grown. Kime tells me, "All of these things have their hard moments. *But,* I really do believe if you have a calling deep inside you -- something you know you're supposed to do and won't stop until you've done it -- that in itself is a success."

As Kime's business grows, she works hard to stay true to her brand. "As a company grows, so do the voices around it. There are more and more opinions about who and what the brand should be, how it should operate, and what its goals should be." As Kime has moved from a one-woman show to managing a team of people, she knows that part of her role is to lead her staff along a path that aligns with her business strategy. Kime also tells me that impacting others in a positive way has become more of a priority each year. She says, "We want to inspire people with not only beautiful things, but also in how we run our business, empower our employees (including working moms), give back to our community and, when possible, use trade and manufacturing as a way of investing in impoverished communities." Kime believes that substantive business practices continue to be a growing and ever-evolving aspect of her brand story.

Kime says the best piece of advice she has received still rings true. "If you build it, they will come. Starting your own company is like the bridge in Indiana Jones -- you have to step out where there's nothing, then the next plank appears just in time!"

Kime's advice to young entrepreneurs: "Find a group of key people that are smarter than you, and have them commit to this journey with you. Even a couple of hours a month can really help a young entrepreneur avoid some key mistakes and setbacks."

www.katiekime.com

# Ann Yancy

RO SHAM BEAUX

When I first met "Mama Beaux" (as I affectionately call Ann Yancy), she was climbing up a ladder hanging lights in her temporary booth at AmericasMart in Atlanta. Our booth was right across from hers, and I beelined right over to introduce myself. I was struck by the gorgeous recycled glass and multi-colored beads of her signature chandeliers that glimmered in the light of her booth. It was like candy hanging from the ceiling! I left that show with Ro Sham Beaux's signature Malibu pendant light loaded into my trunk. It now hangs in the sunroom of my home, and I smile every time I look at it.

Raised in Asheville, North Carolina, Yancy studied sculpture, metalsmithing, and jewelry-making at the Portland School of Art. Jewelry design led her into bespoke lighting designs fashioned from beautiful baubles and beads. After settling in Charleston, South Carolina, Yancy launched Ro Sham Beaux in 2010. Her husband, Will Rogers, soon followed as the CFO into what is now the family business.

In the beginning, the doubters told her, "You will only get so far with two kids!" Yancy loves a challenge. She somehow seems to juggle everything to make it work. As she says, "It takes a village," and Ann's parents were great mentors to her. They worked together her whole life and taught her a terrific work ethic. "They left me with a great sense of confidence that you can achieve most things if you work hard and believe in what you are doing."

As the Ro Sham Beaux brand grows, Ann and her team constantly struggle with keeping up with production. Yancy states, "It's a good problem to have, but also very stressful." Their first year in business they were focused on lighting. Now the product line has expanded to casegoods and a few key upholstered pieces. Yancy and her husband both love the design process and know the company is only as good as the new designs they are able to offer. Ro Sham Beaux products can be seen in some of the finest stores, homes and restaurants from Southampton, to Beverly Hills, to the Grand Cayman Islands.

Yancy's advice to budding entrepreneurs: "Stay open to change. What you may have envisioned for your company will usually evolve into something slightly different."

www.ro-sham-beaux.com

# Beth Lacefield

LACEFIELD

I have long been a fan of Lacefield textiles. Their beautiful patterns and vast array of original designs blow me away. I'm completely obsessed with their Zebra pattern in the Marina colorway. Earlier this year I put it on *everything* including our Kings Grant Chairs in our new office in Charleston, SC. I can't get enough! Although she started as a small handmade home decor products line back in 1996, Beth Lacefield and her team have become a little powerhouse of design. While many big fabric houses are outsourcing manufacturing overseas, Lacefield handles all design, production, and distribution in-house at their Atlanta based headquarters.

Known in the industry for her keen eye for trend setting designs, Lacefield has branched into many licensing projects over the years. Highlights include a very successful rug, pillow, and pouf line with Surya and table and floor lamps for Gallery Designs Lighting. An artist at heart, Lacefield received her degree in Furnishings and Interiors from the University of Georgia. After successful stints as a commercial designer and mural artist after school, Lacefield honed her skills with color and texture working under famed Atlanta fashion designer, Carolyn Tanner in the late 80s and early 90s. On starting Lacefield she says, "I had a strong internal pull for something to call my own. I wanted to share my aesthetic and creative output with others. With my experience in fashion, I understood the importance of details and quality." Undoubtedly this has played a major role in differentiating the Lacefield line from others in the marketplace.

Lacefield has been in the game much longer than other newer textile lines, and she tells me her success has been built on not being afraid to fail or to try new things. She says, "I believe failures are important components of learning and growing, both professionally and personally. In the end what could be considered a failure often helps build one's road to success." What Lacefield is really passionate about is the design part of her business, while manufacturing and sourcing materials is a constant challenge. She says, "Finding domestic resources is difficult, but we are committed to manufacturing our products in the U.S." While so many manufacturers moved their operations overseas back in the late 90s, it's refreshing to see a company like Lacefield that has stayed the course.

Lacefield admits that being pulled into the day-to-day aspects of running the business is a constant balancing act. She has hired a seasoned and capable team to manage the operations part of her business. Lacefield says, "Doing what you love is an immeasurable gift. I must constantly remind myself that the future is bigger than just the one small task at hand. I have to continue to focus on the horizon in order to secure our future growth."

Thinking of starting your own company? Lacefield's advice is, "to surround yourself with people who reflect attributes that you would like in yourself. The power of positive influence is undeniable."

www.lacefielddesigns.com

# Lauren Renfrow

TIMES TWO DESIGN

This eclectic, avant-garde accessories and furniture company
is born out of owner Lauren Renfrow's love of nature's beauty.
Renfrow majored in Environmental Studies and Botany at the
University of Colorado at Boulder before launching a home-based
floral and event design company in Dallas, Texas a few years later.
She quickly became recognized for her signature quartz and citrine
crystals that she added to her floral designs. People responded with
excitement, which led Renfrow to play around with the idea for a
handcrafted quartz lamp. In 2012, she finally turned her inspiration
into reality with the launch of Times Two Design. The line is a
powerhouse of beautiful objects, handcrafted from agate, pyrite,
quartz, stones, glass, antlers, and more.

As the Times Two Design brand continues to grow, Renfrow is focusing more on sculptural and furniture categories and the continued expansion of her tabletop and gift lines. "I am a sculptor at heart and rely on my artistic inspirations to create new products and categories." She believes that creativity, hard work, and focus on excellent customer service have been key to the success of her business. "I listen to customer feedback. Knowing what your customers want can be the difference between success and failure."

In the beginning, Renfrow was often questioned if the long hours she invested in her new company would actually pay off. "In the early days, the business always came first. This meant much less free time for me." Despite the long hours, Renfrow says she will take this any day over a "corporate America job". "I can't sit all day at a desk; I would much rather be working with my hands."

One of the biggest hurdles Renfrow faced early on was ensuring that she sourced the right suppliers for her raw materials. As she says, "creating something once is easy, but reproducing it again and again can be impossible without the right materials." As her business grows and production increases, Renfrow is challenged with maintaining the original character and quality of her products. As a result, her team recently moved into a studio where they manufacture everything in-house. This has helped Renfrow ensure that her products always meet her high-quality standards before shipping to a customer.

Renfrow's advice to those interested in starting a business: "Work hard, stay positive, never stop creating, listen to your clients, and always be an original."

www.timestwodesign.com

# Susan Hornbeak-Ortiz

SHINE BY S.H.O.

Susan Hornbeak-Ortiz came across my radar on Instagram. My mouth fell open at the sight of her Raoul Chair, which takes its cues from the same mid-century point of reference as the Taylor Burke Home Hollings Chair. Hornbeak-Ortiz's chair is stunning. I needed to know more about this west coast designer with serious design chops. I love her bold take on furniture design, and her overall aesthetic is right up my alley!

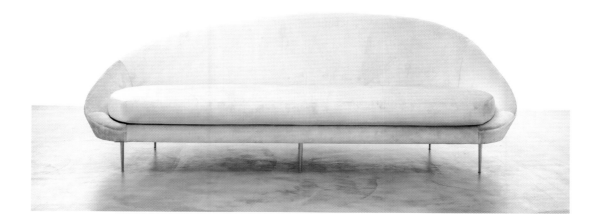

Started in 2004, Shine by S.H.O. is a home decor brand specializing in luxury upholstery, casegoods, rugs, art and lighting. In addition to the company's flagship furniture showroom at the Laguna Design Center, they also offer commercial and residential interior design services. Hornbeak-Ortiz is involved in numerous successful licensing deals with companies such as Z Gallerie, Lino Textiles of New York, Amazon.com's MyHabit and an exclusive Shine by S.H.O. line for The Gilt Groupe.

The name "Shine" comes from a dream involving her grandfather in which he encouraged her to start her own business. Hornbeak-Ortiz says, "I woke up on fire knowing exactly what I wanted to do!" Already in talks with her husband about moving from Portland, Oregon back to California to be closer to family, the duo brainstormed many company concepts. After deciding on a high-end, bespoke lighting and furniture company, they packed up their kids and left their beautiful home for sunny California skies. Hornbeak-Ortiz says, "We traded a large piece of property, our 401(k) and a secure lifestyle for a small beach house and the roller coaster of starting a business. Many people thought I was nuts!"

Hornbeak-Ortiz immediately burst onto the design scene with a series of hand-painted, mouth-blown glass lamps made from early to mid-20th century cast iron molds she found in a dusty West Virginia warehouse. The media salivated over her designs, and the following year she launched her first comprehensive line of upholstery, casegoods, art, and home accessories. Hornbeak-Ortiz's designs landed her in high-profile features in magazines such as *O, The Oprah Magazine. Elle Décor* placed the designer's Lille Dining Table on its annual Top 10 List.

Hornbeak-Ortiz credits her mother, a former interior designer, with teaching her everything she knows about design. She says, "From a very young age I sat in on design meetings, walked job sites and looked at floor plans with her. I still love the smell of old school blueprints!"

Hornbeak-Ortiz makes no apologies for her fashion forward aesthetic. "My designs are not cookie cutter or mainstream. I simply cannot design that way; it is not in my DNA." Hornbeak-Ortiz knows that a certain part of selling her aesthetic is educating the consumer on the higher prices associated with bespoke, custom products that are made locally. She says this can be challenging, "especially in a world full of Pottery Barn and Ikea!" We both agree there is nothing wrong with these companies, people! Don't send us hate mail.

Ready to make your mark on the design industry? Hornbeak-Ortiz's says, "What the world needs are more visionaries! A certain amount of dreaming and naiveté are important in making the leap. Nobody really tells you how deep and bitterly cold the water is, and even if they try to, don't listen!"

www.shinebysho.com

# Lindsay Cowles

## LINDSAY COWLES DESIGNS

I first became aware of Lindsay Cowles when I saw Mandy Rye's (www.waitingonmartha.com) vignette at the ADAC Atlanta Food & Wine Festival in May 2015. Rye chose Cowles' gorgeous wallpaper for the backdrop in her vignette.  I was instantly smitten. Shortly thereafter, we kept popping up in the same social media posts for the Hamptons Designer Show House. Denise McGaha selected Cowles' pillow and my Hollings chairs for her bedroom in the 2015 Show House. Her abstract art printed pillow took center stage in McGaha's grand bedroom and your eye couldn't help but be drawn to it. I had to find out more about this talented lady.

As a young girl, Cowles dreamed of having her own business. She spent many hours painting, creating and letting her imagination run wild, but she never imagined that she could have a business doing just that! After an initial attempt at pre-med at the University of Virginia (Cowles says, "dissections weren't my thing!"), she found herself studying Modern European History, a passion of hers. Upon graduation, the energy and creativity of New York City drew her north and fashion became her creative outlet. She spent the next seven years learning the about the of the sales side of the fashion industry. Cowles found a new love for fabrics while working at Alberta Ferretti and began thinking creatively about how to incorporate her artwork into textiles.

In 2008, Cowles moved to Los Angeles in the midst of the economy slump. Jobs were scarce. Time was plentiful. Cowles spent a lot of time soul searching; trying to figure out the next step in her career. On a trip home to visit family, Cowles watched her sister experiment with painting textured pieces for her senior art project. "I was immediately hooked. I hopped into the car and went to get my own supplies… painting made me feel whole again." That was it. Cowles returned to LA. She worked during the day and spent her evenings and weekends painting. People started asking to buy her work and her business started growing. So, Cowles packed up and moved back to her hometown of Richmond, VA to paint full time. She has never looked back.

Since starting her company, Cowles has expanded into giclee prints, wallcoverings, textiles, ceramic tiles, pillows, and more. She says, "each product is created from a pattern which originates from my paintings. Art is the foundation of my brand."

Figuring out how to market her brand has been one of the biggest challenges for Cowles in launching her business. Over the last year, Cowles has expanded into representation at key showrooms, which takes some of the burden of selling off of her shoulders.

She believes that determination, creativity, and excellent customer service are the key to success. Cowles creates an experience with her customers. She says, "I have structured my business so that I get to interact with each customer who purchases my work. I get to know my clients and experience their joy first hand. I love that!"

Cowles' advice to young entrepreneurs: "Stay focused. Stay driven. Stay passionate."

www.lindsaycowles.com

# Mandy Kellogg Rye

## WAITING ON MARTHA

Mandy Rye and I met at my first tradeshow in Atlanta in 2012. I had just launched Taylor Burke Home and Rye had recently launched her lifestyle blog, *Waiting on Martha*. We still laugh to this day at how I inquired about Martha. I asked, "Is that your mom?" In the same manner, Rye inquired about Burke. Although *Waiting on Martha* was originally founded as a lifestyle blog, the brand has quickly grown to include an e-commerce lifestyle boutique. Rye has also ventured into styling and design, and has created a sister company named Mandy Kellogg Rye Styling + Design.

Rye's business started with boredom and a bracelet. After years of working in the healthcare industry, Rye began making bracelets in her free time as a means to fuel her creativity. Friends and family responded with excitement for her creations, and she started a blog to share her passion. Rye knew from the beginning that she needed to craft a brand story that would stand out. Rye says, "Blogs are born everyday; beautifully styled images are constantly shared on social media. There are more e-commerce boutiques than I can count!" Rye had to figure out early on how to make people take notice of *Waiting on Martha*. They did this through

thoughtful and purposeful imagery. "From day one I worked closely with professional photographers to capture captivating and standout images." That work has paid off.

As Rye's company gained momentum, she struggled with saying no to projects. Rye has to be extremely conscientious about her time and carefully considers what projects she should accept. When evaluating a new project, Rye says, "I always consider two things: is it something I'm passionate about and will it help grow my brand? If it doesn't meet those two criteria, then it takes a back seat."

Rye has learned some personal lessons along the way about setting boundaries and friendships in the industry. "Someone once told me there are friends, and then there are industry friends. You'd be well-served to know and differentiate between the two." Rye keeps this advice close to heart and has learned to protect her best interests.

Rye's advice to up and coming entrepreneurs: "Don't do it unless you love and believe in what you are doing! Otherwise, it's a waste of time, and time is something I never have enough of. *Lastly,* always remember that comparison is the thief of joy. Focus on yourself and your own accomplishments."

www.waitingonmartha.com

# Victoria Larson

VICTORIA LARSON

Victoria Larson is known for her stunning screen-printed textiles that tell stories of wanderlust, lazy days in the garden, and the constant lure of the sea. Her stardust pattern in a beautiful shade of deep navy danced across my Pinterest screen one night, and I was immediately mesmerized. The photograph was styled with a beautiful, gold-leaf oyster shell to accent her textile in the background. I couldn't take my eyes off of it; I wanted to know more.

Like many artists, Larson didn't realize her true talent until after she did some soul searching. An interior designer by trade, Larson took some time off to take care of her young twin daughters. After returning to work years later, Larson found herself feeling a bit unfulfilled and uninspired in the career she once loved. "I realized that instead of selecting color and design from someone else's palette, I needed to be creating my own," says Larson. She began painting again, and the passion and spark for creativity returned as a full-fledged fire. Artist friends introduced her to block printing and sublimation printing, which blended so beautifully with her art. "I began experimenting with creating my own fabric and making pillows. I finally felt like I was doing what I had always wanted to do."

Once Larson discovered she could combine all of her passions -- art, design and textiles -- she found herself on a new career path. She spent a year and a half researching and learning about printing methods, fabrics, and mills. "I taught myself how to create seamless repeats and how to convert my artwork for the digital print process," Larson. Larson soon discovered talented craftspeople that still screen print fabrics by hand in an old mill in New England. These artisans hand-mix color in big pots, then expertly apply the color to silk screens to print flawless designs. "I knew I had to be a part of the textile world!"

Larson's husband, Chris, is the one who gave her the final push to go for it. "He wondered out loud if I was just going to continue playing around with sampling forever." Larson likens this feeling to standing on the dock before you jump in. She says, "You know you want to. You know you are going to, and you know the water is going to be icy cold. You brace yourself, take a deep breath, and then hurdle yourself into the air. The water is cold, but only for a minute. Then you swim out into the deep without looking back."

Reflecting back, Larson confesses to launching her first collection before she was truly ready. "I was so smitten with the process that I wanted to print every design I developed. I was all over the place!" She knew her first collection lacked cohesion, as she was still formulating what she wanted her brand to be. Larson quickly regrouped and began working with a brand coach. She introduced a new website and realized the importance of telling her story. Larson's re-launch had a much more focused message with consistent images to home in on her target market.

Larson tells me that her ability to forge relationships with other industry creatives has strengthened her business, and more importantly, her soul. She has also connected with other women entrepreneurs in her community to form a Mastermind group. "We come from different backgrounds, and each of us brings our own set of business challenges and skills to the table. This group fills a void for me and acts as a sounding board. They supply an unending supply of positive energy."

Larson says she truly loves what she does -- that's what keeps her going. As a small business owner, "the ups are mine alone to savor, but the downs have sometimes made me consider quitting." But Larson knows it's important for her daughters to see that persistence pays off and that it is worth the sacrifice to follow your passion. "If you are determined, you will always find a way to make it work."

Larson believes her success is due to good old-fashioned hard work and determination. Larson knows the competitive environment she plays in and understands the necessity to stay current. She says, "with the advances in technology as well as the rediscovery of artisan techniques, there has been an explosion of new fabric and wall product lines." Larson strives to grow smart, not necessarily big. That means she has had to learn that she can't be everything to everyone. "I've had to narrow my focus to what Victoria Larson the brand does well, even when that limits what Victoria Larson the person has to offer." Larson now sets limits, sticks to what she does best, and hires out the rest.

Larson's advice to budding entrepreneurs: "Just do it! Make a plan and jump in. You will never feel fully ready-- just be ready enough. *And* be prepared to work like you've never worked before. You will never regret following your passion." Larson also urges anyone starting their own business to do their homework to understand the market. "Go through some strategic branding exercises so that you can be clear on how you want to present yourself to the world. Find a mentor early on even if that means hiring a coach." This will be money well spent and will help avoid costly mistakes. Most importantly, "Remember to feed your creative soul. Don't forget to do the thing that drove you to start the business in the first place!"

www.victoria-larson.com

# Jamie Dietrich

## JAMIE DIETRICH DESIGNS

Jamie Dietrich came across my radar when I first saw her gorgeous recycled glass bottle sculptures in her showroom at Atlanta market. I have admired her work for quite some time and was so excited to hear how she got started in the business.

A Southern California native, Dietrich's love for the sea and casual beach living can be seen in her beautiful hand-crafted products. She says, "It all started as a hobby." While growing up near the Rose Bowl Flea Market, Dietrich became a collector of vintage bottles and flea market finds. This was the spark for the launch of her company, Jamie Dietrich Designs, in 2005.

Dietrich's hand-crafted designs of vintage bottles, combined with soldered geodes, crystals and natural sea life, very quickly caught the attention of magazines such as *InStyle, House Beautiful, Elle Décor,* and *Architectural Digest.* Each piece is unique, hence the allure from designers searching for one-of-a-kind products. Designers flocked to the brand, prompting Dietrich to expand her product line. In 2010, she co-founded a new company, Grace & Blake, an eclectic home furnishings and accessories line. Grace & Blake blends materials such as acrylic, vintage textiles, woods and metals to create a clean and modern aesthetic.

Dietrich tells me that motivation and a true love for design have been the keys to her success. Some of Dietrich's friends and family didn't understand her concept and vision when she first started. "I had an idea, and knew I would succeed and persevere. I never quit."

As with many U.S. based companies, Dietrich has struggled with domestic manufacturing to keep pricing competitive with overseas production. Dietrich faced a few bumps in the road to her success. She recalls stocking up on way too much inventory when the economy bottomed out in 2008. "I should have tested the market first before buying that much inventory." At tradeshows you will find Dietrich firmly planted in her showroom ready to meet with customers. She believes those strong relationships have been key to growing her brand. "My favorite part of the business is the daily interactions I have with my customers. I am beyond grateful for those relationships."

Dietrich's advice to budding entrepreneurs: "Never give up on your dream and vision. Believe in yourself and always go with your gut."

www.jamiedietrich.com
www.graceandblake.net

# Lynai Jones

## MITCHELL BLACK

Having spent 20 years after college balancing her corporate career and caring for her four children, Lynai Jones found herself as a homemaker with boundless energy and a penchant for home decor. Jones has had an affinity for fine stationery and cards since she was a small child. "I still have the birthday cards that I've received over the years since I was two!" After meeting two interior designers with a similar eye for style, Mitchell Black was born as a collection of images for letterpress stationery, note cards, wall art, and home decor.

The design aesthetic of Mitchell Black is a modern take on vintage engravings and etchings. At the line's launch most of the collection had a strong royal theme. Since then, Jones has worked with her team to expand and develop curated collections that complement various home decorating styles.

Jones says, "Starting any business takes a leap of faith." She realized early on that while she loved the product and knew it was of the highest quality, it would not be a viable business without the buy-in of the marketplace. Jones says, "I chose to sell at the most heavily attended trade shows for the industry, despite the higher cost to do so compared to the smaller regional shows." Jones knew if she could gain the attention of the big retailers, designers and national magazines she was targeting, Mitchell Black had a chance to thrive. The company gained over 400 customers in its first two years in the market. It is now found in the some of the finest hotels, spas, retailers and luxury stores in the world.

Jones pulled from personal finances to start Mitchell Black, and says, "Financing a business is always tricky and can be the difference between success and failure. Managing the timing of cash flow is necessary for securing supplier and labor in advance to ensure the timely delivery of our product." Jones has kept a keen eye on cash flow and revenue growth in order to prepare for fluctuations in her business.

Jones says that flexibility and relationships are the keys to the company's success. "We have been fortunate to create partnerships in the early stages of the business that continue to benefit the brand in many ways such as expanding our sales channels and elevating our marketing." Jones' relationships range from well-known, high-end designers and retailers to artisans and business owners worldwide.

Delivering on time has been a key component to establishing Mitchell Black's reputation in the industry, but "no one builds a successful business without snags in the plan or problems along the way," says Jones. One of the biggest issues she encountered in the early stages was accurately predicting demand. As a company that both manufactures in-house and designs product made by outside vendors, her team keeps some amount of product on hand. Jones recalls a costly mistake she made by following an employee's unsubstantiated sales estimates that led her to purchase 70,000 envelopes and 110,000 cards. "For a start-up paper line, those numbers were outrageous! Lesson learned -- research the market demand in your business space. Find the low volume suppliers, and know that sometimes it is better to pay a higher price for lower initial quantities until you know which of your products are the true winners worth the space and money needed to keep inventory." Jones learned to always follow her own gut and not someone else's.

Jones' style is to jump into things head first, but she acknowledges this can be emotionally draining, expensive and very risky. She says, "I do believe in business you are either all in or you are out." This is advice she would share with those looking to get started. For Jones, the regret of not giving it her all would be far worse than the regret of not having ever tried to make it a success.

www.mitchellblack.com

# Lori Dennis and Kelli Ellis

DESIGN CAMPUS

I first met Lori Dennis and Kelli Ellis at High Point Market after they received a press package from us before the show. It was a simple package of Goo Goo Clusters with a hand-written note from me stating, "we can't wait to show you our new "Goo"dies at market!" I was so impressed that these busy ladies personally came into our showroom to thank us for this small gesture. They were so kind and gracious, and I was enamored with their confidence and feel-good vibes. These were strong women not afraid to help other women succeed. My kind of ladies!

Kelli Ellis Interior Design

If you have attended any of the various furniture and home decor trade shows around the country, inevitably you've seen the fabulous duo behind the renowned workshop Design Campus. Design Campus is a two-day seminar for interior designers and design lovers presented by Dennis and Ellis. These ladies are spearheading the movement to give back to the design community in a dynamic, refreshing and real way. Internationally known by their appearances on HGTV, Bravo, NBC, Oxygen, TLC and Food Network, not to mention the numeous articles in various publications, Dennis and Ellis have spent decades educating designers and design enthusiasts about interior design basics and more. On top of that, both are published authors! Dennis wrote Green Interior Design, filled with comprehensive resources and tools for sustainable design. Ellis wrote *Do I Look Skinny in This House?*, based on her love for design psychology and the subsequent certified coaching program she created. Dennis and Ellis proudly serve as brand ambassadors, furniture and product designers, public speakers and mentors to the design community.

Lori Dennis Interior Design

Interior designers in their own right, both of these powerhouses started their successful interior design firms in the late 1990s. The idea of Design Campus started in 2012 when Dennis and Ellis both participated as speakers on a panel for "Influential Women in Design" at Las Vegas market. As the ladies shared their experiences and knowledge and fielded questions from the audience, they realized the synergy between them was powerful. The women were energized by how engaged the audience was during their panel discussion. Dennis says, "a couple of margaritas later and a trip to the ladies room (where most meetings are held!)", this dynamic duo cooked up what soon became Design Campus. Nine months later they launched their first seminar in Austin, Texas and have never looked back.

Design Campus has now evolved into an online resource for the architectural and design community. People are able to watch content in the comfort of their own office as well as communicate and engage with others in their field. Both ladies are proud to have changed the way designers communicate, conduct business and collaborate.

Lori Dennis Interior Design

Ellis has been surrounded by entrepreneurs her entire life and remembers her rudimentary marketing efforts early in her career. Back in the days before the internet, Ellis used to take out ads in the local newspaper. She says, "I hit the ground running in high heels, but I ran like Forrest Gump!" She relied on her family and friends when needed and says her father always gave her great advice. Ellis remembers, "He always said to me, don't be the assistant; be the boss! You are the boss!" That vote of confidence from her father has kept with her throughout her career.

Dennis has also had the support of her family and friends her entire career. She admits that the 2008 economic change threw her for a loop. Dennis says, "When the downturn happened, I had to lay off my help and start all over." Dennis refocused her energy on writing her book, *Green Interior Design,* and spending time with her newborn daughter. In hindsight, the timing was perfect.

As a result of the exposure from their interior design work and Design Campus, both Dennis and Ellis have secured successful licensing deals. Dennis holds product licenses with Jaipur Rugs, Tile Bar and Casa Catorce Furniture & Fabrics. Ellis has also licensed many products including her own line with Tile Bar, outdoor rugs and lighting, and is currently creating an art glass collection with Frates.

Dennis and Ellis are both huge proponents of the "just do it" mentality. Ellis urges young entrepreneurs to "follow your passion and create a career around it." Dennis adds, "Get a great internship." Both of these ladies are paving the way for interior designers to connect and collaborate on a level that was non-existent before Design Campus. Find and attend one of their live events at www.designcampus.com

www.kelliellis.com   www.loridennis.com

www.designcampus.com

# Rivers Spencer

## RIVERS SPENCER COLLECTION

Rivers Spencer's line of metal, upholstery, accent pieces, and casegoods is both timeless and elegant. The hand-finished gold and silver leafing she uses on many of her pieces truly makes her collection a work of art. Who would have known that this design dynamo started out her career studying to become a lawyer! Spencer's time spent at her grandmother's in Jackson, Mississippi became the catalyst for her trip down the production development path. Spencer taught herself faux finishing and began practicing on the many pieces of antique furniture in her grandmother's garage. Spencer initially thought of it as a way to work off the stresses of preparing for law school, but she says, "After selling almost an entire house full of furniture at a local antique booth, I knew this was what I was meant to do!"

Spencer soon left the path to law school behind and picked up every interior design book and magazine she could get her hands on to learn the industry. Additional experience was gained traveling to markets throughout the country. She says, "In 2012, I used the money from my antique booth sales and other capital to open a retail showroom offering design services on Magazine Street in New Orleans."

The retail showroom was an immediate success. Spencer soon found herself immersed in interior design projects. These projects led to many requests for custom furniture, and Spencer was hooked. She launched her own line of furniture, the Rivers Spencer Collection, which is bench-made and hand-finished in New Orleans.

Within two years, Spencer outgrew her retail location and renovated her current location, an old double shotgun house in the center of Magazine Street's design district. In her latest venture, Spencer partnered with Tritter Feefer, a made-in-America furniture manufacturer, on a line of fresh, yet classically designed, pieces.

I am struck by how much Spencer has accomplished in her career as she enters her 30s. Breaking into a market in a new city is never easy. Spencer had plenty of people tell her that she didn't have enough experience or that she was too young to start her business. She says, "It only matters what you think you're capable of, and I had no doubt in my ability to make this business successful."

Spencer tells me that grit, determination, a strong work ethic, and an amazing team have been the keys to her success. She says, "You can't grow without the right people, and I'm lucky enough to have the best project manager, store manager and production manager that I could possibly ask for. These individuals allow me to sleep at night, because I know things are taken care of."

As Spencer's business has grown, scaling her business in the right way has been challenging. She says, "It is very difficult to know when to hire someone and how to create a division of labor. Everything is trial and error, and there is a definite transition period of absolute chaos and growing pains." Spencer knows the value in working with vendors and artisans that she trusts. She says, "Blind trust can leave quite a dent in one's bank account. Trust, but verify!"

Thinking of starting your own company? Spencer's advice is, "Don't neglect the business side of your business. The way you operate the back end of your business ultimately leads to the level of success you are able to achieve."

www.riversspencer.com

# Cari Cucksey

## REPURPOSE RECOLOR

Could the title, "Cash & Cari" on HGTV be any more cute? The show caught my attention back in 2011 as I watched the talented Cucksey search through homes looking for items to sell or refurbish as she prepared the home for a huge estate sale. It was quite entertaining! The show enjoyed a solid run on HGTV, and is now in reruns on the W Network, Choice TV, and the History Channel in 40 countries around the world. The "Cash & Cari" experience led Cucksey to other business ventures and to develop products with the refurbisher and do-it-yourself (DIY) customer in mind. She now has a paint & stain product line specifically made with the DIYer in mind. Cucksey's RePurpose ReColor™ has made a splash with DIY bloggers and Pinterest followers alike as a product line perfect for individuals looking to save money on quick home decor updates.

Cucksey's desire to start her own business began at an early age. "I had a paper route when I was eleven years old. I wasn't exactly honest about my age so that I could get the job!" Cucksey credits her parents as early mentors and she tells me they strongly encourage her entrepreneurial spirit. "They always told me that whatever I did, I should do it well." Both of Cucksey's parents and grandparents are collectors and she has been around the antiques world her entire life. Cucksey tells me she shares their love of history and all things old. She says, "My grandfather had a knack for repurposing things and that certainly rubbed off on me as a young child. He was the original 'American Picker!'" Referencing the History Channel's popular show, Cucksey has also ridden the popular wave of a renewed interest in repurposing and antiques. With RePurpose ReColor, Cucksey has utilized her knowledge combined with an increase in public demand for repurposed products to create a successful business venture.

Cucksey now has her hands full with a multitude of business ventures including running estate sales and operating her vintage store, RePurpose. Not to mention refurbishing just about anything she can get her hands on! Cucksey says

that growing pains have been her biggest challenge with the expansion of her business opportunities. She tells me that time management has been essential to her business. "Hiring a bookkeeper and delegating administrative activities has helped streamline my business. I realized I can't do everything and there are only so many hours in the day."

Cucksey also tells me that managing staff is her most difficult task as business owner. "Who you hire to represent your brand is very important as well as having a loyal team. Hiring your friends may seem like a good idea, but is not always the best choice!"

Cucksey's advice to budding entrepreneurs is, "Follow your passion! Surround yourself with successful people who can help you along the way. Ideas are great, but they require action and execution. You can either be a dreamer or a doer. Life is short and the only risk is not taking any. Just go for it!"

www.repurposeshop.com

# Maggie Mielczarek

## LELAND GAL

The first time I saw the Leland Gal logo, with a tree as the backdrop to the text, I knew there had to be a story. I love how Maggie Mielczarek talks about the fact that she stared at this Cherry Tree through the window of her grandparents, and now her parents, house in Leland, Michigan. It's a testament to her love of nature and her strong sense of family ties. Mielczarek's ever-growing textile company boasts patterns that portray a breezy, laidback lifestyle. Many of them are quite cheeky and trick the eye. Who knew that birch trees, boat oars, and fish could be used in a way to create fun geometric patterns? As you look closely, the patterns make you smile when you realize the basis of the print.

After teaching for over 10 years in Chicago, Mielczarek's family moved to Grand Rapids, Michigan where she started a new job as an art teacher. Mielczarek had to learn a new graphic design software program as part of her new job curriculum. She says, "I fell in love with this new medium. I found myself spending all of my available free time learning how to create patterns from my existing art." After a few shows and positive feedback, Mielczarek decided to open her storefront in Leland, Michigan. They carry a wide array of bright, fun, coastal inspired designs and finished products for the home.

Mielczarek says, "This new career path has afforded me the chance to feel completely fulfilled as an artist, a business owner, and as a member of a community that holds a special place in my heart."

As part of the process of opening her storefront, Mielczarek had to submit a detailed business plan. In hindsight she says this is one of the best things she did early on. "While writing a business plan was not my idea of fun, it gave me the chance to map out how I would ideally envision the future of my business. My business plan has become my greatest asset as I reference it when developing new products."

Both of Mielczarek's parents were entrepreneurs, and she had the full support of her husband to start her company. However, as Mielczarek says, "A lot of people thought it was foolish for me to quit my teaching job in order to pursue Leland Gal full time." As she says, "[it made me] more available and more involved. I wanted to see my creative passion grow. I knew I would never forgive myself if I didn't at least try."

One of the biggest challenges Mielczarek faced early on was editing herself. She started producing too many options and colors for customers. "I realized that is not a successful model. I've learned to focus more on offering fewer items that are on-trend and stay within my brand niche," says Mielczarek. Over time, Mielczarek has learned, and is still learning, how much money and effort to invest into each new idea and when to know when let an idea go.

www.lelandgal.com

150

# Stacy Kunstel

DUNES & DUCHESS

The first time I laid eyes on Stacy Kunstel (a.k.a. Duchy) and Michael Partenio (a.k.a. Dunes), Kunstel looked like a Parisian model in her beautiful Japanese kimono dress, and Partenio looked like he was straight out of Nantucket in his seersucker jacket with a colorful pocket square. They were by far the most interesting exhibitors I had seen at High Point market, and I beelined right into their showroom. Their bright and bold hand-turned candelabras and wall sconces are a sight to behold. *And* those glossy candy-colored finishes! Their design-driven line of casegoods has become a go-to for designers across the country looking for that one statement piece to complete a space.

Kunstel had long dreamed of having her own company. She says, "When the downturn in the housing market and the magazine industry hit around 2009, I really had to ask myself what it was that I wanted to do." Up to that point, Kunstel had only worked in publishing. First as a writer, then as an interiors stylist, Kunstel's resume includes national publications such as *Southern Living, Better Homes & Gardens, Country Living* and *Traditional Home.* Kunstel pondered a fashion-based business, public relations and a number of other things, but it was working on a photo shoot that determined Kunstel's next move both professionally and personally. She says, "Michael (Partenio) spotted an antique candelabra that he wanted to recreate for me as a show of his affection. I fell in love, bought a vacation home, and then started a company with him in August 2010. His act of affection ignited an entire business and dozens of products, showing me once again that love and creativity go hand in hand."

Each product in the Dunes & Duchess line is made in and ships from their Connecticut workshop. Kunstel says, "Manufacturing in the U.S. continues to be a huge challenge, but it is one that we are committed to." Kunstel and Partenio do most of the work in-house so they can control the quality. They both strive for very high standards, and not everyone is up to the task. Kunstel says, "We receive pieces of turned wood, and we sand, glue, prime, paint, and assemble them in our Connecticut workshop." This tight control over production ensures a consistent product each and every time.

Kunstel says the biggest challenge they face as their business grows is offloading some of the operational activities to others. "We are truly do-it-yourselfers. We do our own public relations, marketing, photography, social media, shipping and billing. We wear all the hats, yet the business has grown beyond our capacity to do so." Kunstel has faced the same challenges we all face as our small companies grow to include staff and managing other people. She admits to a tough learning curve without any mentors to help pull her along. She says, "We know the tough road of starting and running your own company. We try to share as much knowledge as we can to help others wanting to do the same."

Dunes & Duchess products have been in dozens of magazines in the last few years. Kunstel believes that each of their products adds joy and beauty to their customers' lives. The product line has stayed true to the Dunes & Duchess brand story from the beginning. "There's no mistaking our lacquer finishes or eye-popping colors for anything other than a Dunes & Duchess piece," says Kunstel. Some designers even refer to their products as iconic in form. Kunstel loves to see their pieces mixed in different ways to create unique and interesting spaces. She says, "It's pretty amazing that we make things from wood and turn them into a little piece of wonderful. We make beauty, and it is exactly what we intend on continuing to do."

Thinking of starting your own company? Kunstel's advice is to "become an expert in what you do, and believe that no one can do it as well as you can. I know everyone says you have to have passion and you have to work hard, but above all you have to believe in what you're doing."

www.dunesandduchess.com

# Mary Catherine Folmar

COTTON + QUILL

The first time I laid eyes on this sweet little Alabama beauty was back in April, 2013 at High Point Market. Mary Catherine Folmar waltzed right into my showroom to show me her new fabric collection. I was blown away by her designs. I knew her business had just launched back in 2012. We formed a fast friendship of kindred spirits supporting each other as our brands grew. Through some creative thinking, Taylor Burke Home and Cotton + Quill have shown together at several markets in High Point and Atlanta. I have personally enjoyed watching her soar as her brand has grown over the last couple of years.

Initially launched as a pillow and soft goods line, Cotton + Quill has quickly expanded into cut yardage, custom pillows, wallpaper, and trimmings. As the creative force behind Cotton + Quill, Folmar hand-illustrates each of her designs. Let me repeat -- she hand-illustrates, people! From my perspective, Folmar's brand power is based in her intellectual property. She will tell you that determining cost and price points were the hardest part for her in entering the market. How do you value the intellectual property of your own designs when you are just starting out? Folmar has learned along the way, but this was a major challenge for her when she first started.

As the Cotton + Quill brand and business has grown, Folmar has faced challenges in staffing up and knowing when to do it. Her biggest challenge is, "not having ten of me! When I first started I did everything from marketing and accounting to design and production. Trying to keep up with everything in a timely manner has been the hardest part as my company has grown."

Quality control has been a valuable lesson for Mary Catherine as her business has grown as well. "Drop-shipping product directly from my manufacturer without being able to have an extra layer of quality control has created some costly mistakes. I learned that mistakes happen and it is all about how you handle the situation that leaves your customer with a good or bad impression of Cotton + Quill."

Folmar's advice to budding entrepreneurs is, "don't expect a paycheck or vacation for awhile, but don't give up! If you're passionate about what you do, then think about what you're doing as a business rather than a hobby. This creates a mindset for success."

www.cottonandquill.com

# Sherrill Canet

## SHERRILL CANET INTERIORS, LTD.

Sherrill Canet's story started on the runway. Her early modeling career in New York quickly took her to London where she found herself surrounded by a treasure trove of markets and antiques. Canet juggled modeling gigs while attending design school during her time in London. She says, "Antique shopping could be done everyday of the week in all corners of the city and countryside. I was hooked!" Armed with a container load of antiques, Canet returned to the U.S. and opened her first antique shop, Bellwether Antiques.

Canet soon found herself immersed in interior design jobs. She says, "Clients would come into my shop, admire the aesthetic, and ask for help in their homes and offices." Canet maintained two locations in New York, Manhattan and Locust Valley, while servicing clients from all over the country and abroad. "I found the design end of maintaining and displaying my inventory extremely gratifying, and my interior design business went hand in hand with my retail stores. Not to mention, I had an excuse to keep shopping for beautiful things!"

Canet says her brand story shifted as she began to custom design furniture and carpets for clients. Thrusting herself into the show house circuit, Canet's high profile work began to draw national attention, and her custom-designed furniture and carpets received rave reviews from designers and critics. By the way, her emerald sitting room with black, white, and gold accents she designed for her second turn in the Kips Bay Decorator Show House is still one of my all-time favorites. Drop dead gorgeous! Canet says, "The carpet in that room was from my first collection I designed with Stark, called 'Ellipse'. I really love the graphic black and white in that design!"

Most people agree that nothing new is presented either in design or manufacturing without taking a few chances. One of the qualities I love most about Canet is that she is a bit of a risk taker. She tells me, "Creativity has to come with a bit of disregard for the rules. Nothing magical happens without a little risk!" Canet takes a classic idea and makes it fresh by blending periods, styles, shapes, and finishes. Much of her influence comes from her days on the runway. "While working with some of the most talented fashion designers, I was surrounded by scale, beauty, color and restraint." Undoubtedly, Canet's keen eye can be seen in her fashion forward yet classic designs.

Canet's high profile has not escaped a few bumps in the road over the years. As with many designers, her business was hit hard by the downturn in the U.S. economy in 2007/2008. Canet introduced her first furniture line with Stark shortly after the stock market crash. She knew immediately that her timing was off. Canet states, "People were not considering crocodile covered console tables or any luxury goods for that matter. People were worried about paying their bills!" Canet learned a valuable lesson: world and fluctuating market events shape the industry and are often unforeseeable. "It is important to plan for the unexpected."

Canet's ability to be aggressive at the right moments has served her well over the years in enduring the ups and downs of the industry. "Marketing your product successfully is everything in selling and branding. Things don't just happen, you have to make them happen!" Canet has been smart to steadily grow her design business by diversifying with product development. She says, "With my background in antiques and interior design, moving to product development and manufacturing is a good marriage. Having a few related avenues in your business keeps things interesting and doesn't make you reliant on one product or skill."

Thinking of developing your own product? Canet advises, "Have a solid business plan. Making it happen is more than a sketch on paper." She adds, "There is nothing more satisfying that being your own boss!"

www.sherrillcanet.com

# Jill Rosenwald

## JILL ROSENWALD DESIGNS

The first time I heard about Jill Rosenwald was in 2014 while I was visiting one of our customers, Liz Caan's design studio and retail store in Newton, Massachusetts. Caan was just launching a new ceramic collection with Rosenwald. Her new designs were like eye candy to me. Rosenwald's story is as funny as it is inspiring to anyone who wants to start their own business. I love her "get it done" attitude. Rosenwald always liked making and selling odds and ends. She started selling her wares illegally on the streets of Soho in New York City back in the early 1990s. On one of her first days in Soho, two undercover cops stopped and gave her a summons. They took a few items as evidence, and Rosenwald says, "I'm pretty sure they just liked what they saw!" Undeterred, the next day she returned to her favorite corner. "[I was] sandwiched between a lemon ice guy and a crew of street dancers". She loved the energy, and the money in her pocket at the end of each day felt like success.

As Rosenwald says, "At the time, I was on a mission. My then-boyfriend invited me to travel the Greek Islands on his dad's schooner if I could get enough cash to meet them at the port. Bam! That was the spark for my business. [I was] motivated by a dude." She didn't get to Greece, but she did start a business. That brand has still excited and empowered her to this day.

Rosenwald has always loved making beautiful and colorful things. "I love that we make pieces for the smart and stylish people that enjoy them." Her company has evolved since the '90s, starting with clay jewelry that was often lauded as "heavy on the lobes!" Next came wall pieces, and then onto functional pots that are still made today. She dipped her toe into the baby business for a little while, and then made a fast break into licensing in the early 2000s. "I made many mistakes back then, but I am proud to say that our brand in both pottery and textiles is about bold as brass design. We aim to bring a little piece of happy into people's lives."

My eyes bulged when Jill told me about some of the naysayers early in her career. "I had a college ceramics professor who essentially told me my entire senior project was a waste of time. And I was told more than once that I should change my brand name to something less Jew-y." Overall she's been very lucky to have mostly cheerleaders in her court, and wonderful parents who never saw a design of hers without shrieking that she was a genius.

The biggest challenge Rosenwald has faced with her growing business is learning how to get out of the way. She always thought she needed to be in the production line. "I was advised that in order to grow, I would need to step out of the way and let other people do the work of making pieces." Rosenwald realized, "I'm the designer. A designer needs to spend time designing!"

Rosenwald has really found her "jam" as she calls it collaborating with other designers. She has ceramic collections with Erin Gates, Liz Caan and Gray Malin, and continues to expand her licensing deals. As Rosenwald says, "I love making new relationships with fun, delicious, creative people." She hopes to continue making "beautiful life affirming sh*t" as her friend, Jonathan Adler says. I have no doubt that she will.

Rosenwald's advice to anyone thinking of starting a business: "Be good to other people in your field. Be generous. Share, and teach others what you know so they won't make the same mistakes."

www.jillrosenwald.com

# Roxy Te Owens

SOCIETY SOCIAL

Anyone like myself with a penchant for bold color and fresh, design-driven decor knows about Society Social. Either through the many publications that have featured her products, or the social media storm of her shop, Shop Society Social, you can't miss Roxy Te Owens' signature style. Her inspiring photos make you long for the products scrolling before your eyes.

Launched in 2011, Society Social is a lifestyle brand featuring vintage-inspired bar carts and colorful furniture. Owens also created hostess attire that draws from the retro ritual of cocktail hour. The brand has become known for its signature elements such as bright pops of color, faux bamboo, and designer style at approachable price points. The idea for her company started while hosting a cocktail party at her home. Guests oohed and aahed over Owens' stocked bar cart during the event. Additionally, while avidly reading design blogs, Owens noticed everyone seemed to be talking about bar carts, yet there was nowhere to buy them at the time. Society Social was born the following year with the launch of six bar carts.

Owens has always been inspired by life's shared moments, and she tries to put that love into each piece. Owens says, "It's truly an honor to receive notes and photos from my customers such as 'Your Sedgewick bar cart made it just in time for my bridal shower!'" She loves the idea that she gets to contribute to the moments that make life special.

While Owens has had very supportive cheerleaders from her family and friends, she recalls a meeting she had at the start of her career where the tone was more than condescending. "I was talked down to the entire time. It ended with them saying, 'Maybe we'll work with you when you have a real business.' They asked me for the meeting!" Owens shook it off and continued to believe in herself and build her brand.

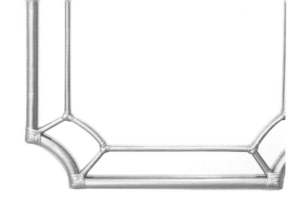

Owens self-funded the startup for Society Social. She couldn't afford a public relations company in the early stages, and she wasn't sure how to get press attention. Therefore, she focused heavily on social media to gain notoriety. Her collaborations with other designers and businesses have garnered major attention. While some people question Owens' willingness to share information with competitors, Owens shrugs it off. "I think there is room for all of us to shine. If you're being smart about it, why not help each other?" Owens believes that collaborations have the potential to increase everyone's success. "Teaming up with people and businesses that have similar interests can be great for cross marketing." She warns, "While it can be fun and inspiring, remember it should also be fair and mutually beneficial for the parties involved."

Owens knows the competitive landscape is more crowded and fiercer than ever. Many would argue this is largely due to the fact that technology and social media make is possible for nearly anyone to start a business and do it fast.

Owens's advice to budding entrepreneurs: "Find a niche and own it. Holding strong to your unique point of view helps you stand out from the hundreds of people who are most likely trying to do the same thing as you."

www.shopsocietysocial.com

# Kat Mulford and Lee Lesley

ADDISON WEEKS

The design duo behind Addison Weeks started as two friends that met as graphic designers right out of college. They successfully launched a jewelry line, Turq, over a decade ago. After closing the business to focus on marriage and children, these ladies reunited with renewed energy to launch Addison Weeks in 2012. They tell me, "We initially started with our logo. We both loved old silver marks that are stamped onto precious pieces. We envisioned our identity stamped into our pieces in a similar fashion. Hopefully our pieces are keepsakes that will last for years as well."

While most people have gotten to know Addison Weeks by their gorgeous jewelry, they are now venturing into home decor. Mulford and Lesley initially launched their collection with a small line of jewelry and clutches. The clutches are all handmade and are beautiful works of art. The women tell me "people would comment on how they wanted to leave our clutches on their living room coffee table because they were so beautiful." This led the ladies into product development for decorative boxes and other home objects. "We have taken an earring and turned it into a drawer pull because of customer feedback. It's so fun to take our aesthetic and expand it into other types of products!"

Having two women at the helm of a ship could be a huge challenge. This business model may not work for everyone, but this duo has found their working groove. Mulford and Lesley know the key to their success is listening to each other. They tell me, "We encourage each other. If we both go home and work on design sketches, we each want to wow the other."

Mulford and Lesley's friends and family have been very supportive in the launch and continued success of Addison Weeks. In the beginning a few people rolled their eyes with a "here they go again" look, but the ladies will tell you, "We had a vision in our heads and no one was stopping that train!" Their biggest challenge right out of the gate was figuring out who they were. They have worked hard to refine their mission, define their target customer and determine how to reach them.

Mulford and Lesley admit that mistakes happen, and how you handle them is what's important. They recall a time when a new employee accidentally charged a customer the amount of her zip code instead of the $200 total. As Kat says, "We are both Southern gals, so we try to have good manners and write nice thank you notes...and sometimes, apology notes!" As for future projects, the duo plans to develop a line of gemstone hardware and expand their successful candle line.

Mulford and Lesley would tell newcomers to "Trust your instincts and don't be afraid to put your ideas out there. Don't waste time second guessing yourself!"

www.addisonweeks.com

# Barbara Cosgrove

BARBARA COSGROVE LAMPS

I was first introduced to Barbara Cosgrove Lamps when I met AJ Cosgrove, Cosgrove's daughter-in-law, at Atlanta market. Over dinner and drinks, I learned the family story behind the brand. This made me fall deeper in love with their gorgeous line of lamps.

Cosgrove started the company in the late 1990s in her garage out of the necessity to create. As a life-long artist holding two masters degrees in sculpture, Cosgrove's creativity was her happy place. Becoming an entrepreneur was an accident! It occurred to Cosgrove that lamps are where form meets function. Cosgrove says, "Lamps are little sculptures that everyone has in their homes." She attended High Point Market one year with a friend and fell in love with the idea of selling lamps as sculpture for the home. "Lamps make a huge difference in the way a room looks, even unlit. Turn them on, and wow!"

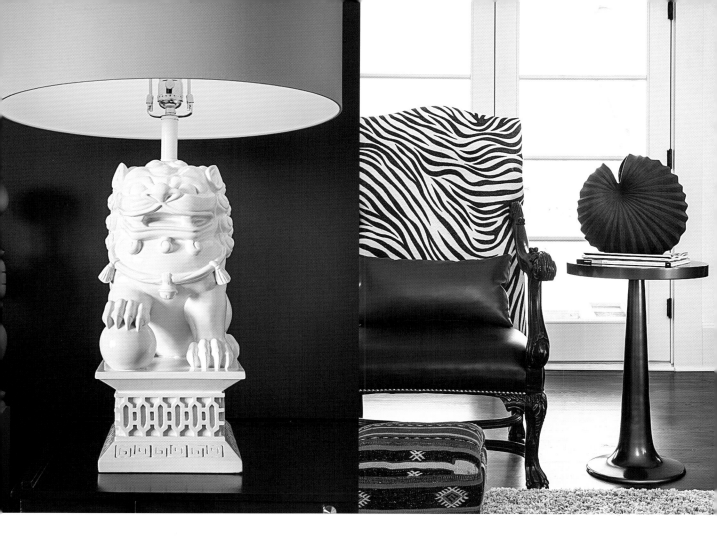

Cosgrove has stayed true to her aesthetic over the years, and the same simple values she started with still hold value. "We believe in timeless, quality product, and we want our customers to love what they buy." The branding has changed slightly as it has become more sophisticated, and social media has become a valuable part of her marketing. Cosgrove has expanded over the years into accessories and fixtures. Interior designers have become the cornerstone of her business, an evolution from the early years when the sole focus was on retail store accounts to get lamps on the floor.

Cosgrove believes having tenacity and avoiding fads have been the keys to her success. "Over the years as the economy has twisted and turned, so did we." Cosgrove currently manufactures 75 percent of the line domestically. She says, "I felt it was important to pull production out of China. Minimum order quantities are outrageous and the quality is plummeting." Like myself, Cosgrove agrees it feels good to support the U.S. economy, stating, "Manufacturing in the U.S. is faster, smaller runs are permitted, better quality is produced, and you receive the product in a timelier manner."

While now revered as a permanent presence in the home decor lamp category, Cosgrove remembers some early, laughable moments that occurred as a new brand on the scene at market. "I remember a designer coming through the showroom with her large entourage, and she actually patted me on the head at market! Another well-known designer told me my clear cords looked cheap, and they should be gold colored instead." Cosgrove brushed off these incidents, and says that the home decor community in general has been extremely supportive.

Cosgrove admits the move from studio artist to businesswoman was confusing at first. She faced a lot of stumbling blocks along the way, including staffing, conquering payroll, receiving loans and developing exhibition manuals and marketing materials. "This kind of stuff really weighed me down!" Once Cosgrove was a regular in the home decor marketplace, her challenge was more about finding her place as a boutique lighting line in the face of many larger, price point driven competitors. Cosgrove has learned to stay focused on what she is doing and not so much on what everyone else is doing. She says, "It has served me well."

Cosgrove is a strong believer in problem solving and figuring things out as she goes along. "If you feel the need for a lot of advice from someone else, then you probably shouldn't go out on your own." From a creative standpoint she "couldn't imagine doing anything else."

Cosgrove's advice to budding entrepreneurs: "Being an entrepreneur is a lot of sleepless nights and long days paying the bills, but it's the best job you will ever have!"

www.barbaracosgrovelamps.com

# Beth Collier

VANCOLLIER

I first met Beth Collier at High Point market and was drawn to her warm and unassuming personality. She has a quiet confidence about her that is refreshing. Every time I see her at market, I love hearing the stories behind each piece she and her husband, Chris, make in their hometown of Washington, North Carolina.

Collier's interior firm was founded in 1995. Her work is influenced by a background in art history and many years spent collecting antiques with her husband. Their first project was renovating the 1907 Georgian-style hospital where his grandfather was a surgeon. Their furniture line was inspired by the Eastern North Carolina landscape -- literally what they could see out their windows including the enormous Ginkgo tree in the courtyard of their home. They set the iconic leaf shape on a curvilinear stem that coiled at the base to create their first piece called the Ginkie Martini Table. The tree's branches inspired their Beebe Cocktail Table, named after their oldest son. Collier has also repurposed tobacco sticks, historically used as stakes for hanging tobacco leaves to dry, into headboards and lighting designs.

The inspiration has produced successive collections. The vanCollier line has grown to include upholstery and mirrors. Collier had to learn profit margins and receivables as she went. "Building the bike while riding the bike", is how Collier describes it. She credits WithIt, a professional women's organization in the home furnishings industry, as her go-to resource for help with business questions and issues faced during her start-up phase. Tackling overseas shipping was another hurdle. An early commission required them to ship a dozen mirrors to London. "That is something that has to be done right or they will arrive in shards, not to mention the potential for decades of bad luck!" All in all, Collier expresses only one major regret: the aftermath of an editorial feature on their Pagoda Lantern. "I wish we had built up inventory as soon as we found out it was going to be featured in *British House & Garden*. We had calls from all over Europe."

Collier owes her success to the fact that their designs appeal to interior designers and architects. "Our gilded and platinum finishes really show the hand and craftsmanship of our pieces." The brand has evolved from Collier designing single statement pieces to creating an environment that reflects their style. In early 2015 Collier was mad about Yves Klein blue, so she sourced ultramarine theatre paint in France. "We splashed it all over everything from sculptures to our Moroccan mirror for the Spring High Point Market. It defined us that season, and it was our most successful trip there by far."

Have ideas for developing your own product? Collier's advice to young entrepreneurs is, "Do what you love. You can't sell product that you wouldn't want to own yourself."

www.vancollier.com

# ML Littlefield

TRITTER FEEFER

When the name "Tritter Feefer" rolls off of your tongue, it definitely brings a smile to your face! I'd say pretty smart branding by Bill Aultman and ML Littlefield for their gorgeous customizable casegoods and accent pieces. What I appreciate the most about their products are the hand-applied, distressed-washed finishes that look perfectly aged to a soft patina. Along with more contemporary finishes, the design aesthetic takes you back to a time of authentic craftsmanship when making furniture by hand was an art. When I walk into their showroom at the Atlanta Decorative Arts Center, managed by their son Rik, it makes me feel very grown up to be surrounded by such timeless classic beauty.

The story of this company starts with a cross-country move. In 2006, after relocating from Colorado to Georgia to be closer to their grandchildren, the couple soon began buying and selling antiques at Scott's Antiques and other Atlanta venues. ML tells me they had no idea that selling at Scott's would lead them to starting their own company. She says, "We knew we were onto something and loved what we were doing. We just kept moving forward." The name Tritter Feefer comes from the nicknames the Bill gave to their newborn grandchildren, Tristan and Faith. She says, "it just stuck."

ML is proud of the company's commitment to sustainable manufacturing principles and their investment in the American workforce. However, she says, "There are so many layers of government regulation on local, state, and national levels with little advocacy to bring production back to the U.S." ML knows domestic manufacturing gives her company the ability to customize their products, and this has allowed them to carve out a nice, niche market for their products. Although customization has become ingrained in their brand story, ML has learned you cannot please everyone. "I committed to a custom design early on that totally exceeded our capabilities. It caused a great deal of grief for me, our staff and eventually the customer. We resolved it, and I've learned not to say yes as easily as I once did."

Now, let's get back to those beautiful finishes! ML and Bill personally developed most of the company's signature custom finishes. The complexity of layers can be experienced on each of their beautiful products. In the beginning, ML received some great advice: "When you've created a new finish, you need to be able to step back and know there's nothing like it in the marketplace. If not, trash it!"

ML's advice to budding entrepreneurs: "There are many internet sites out there that list the traits of successful entrepreneurs, and in many cases those traits won't make you the most popular kid on the playground. Know yourself and be honest with yourself. If you don't have those characteristics, then stick with a cushy desk job! As they say, leaders are born, not made."

www.tritterfeefer.com

# Lucy Smith

## LUCY SMITH DESIGNS

I met Lucy Smith at High Point Market and fell in love with her bold metal tables and their intricate honeycombed design. Then I fell in love with her friendly personality. Her collection of handcrafted metal furnishings is manufactured in Anniston, Alabama where Smith lives. She launched the line in 2009 in collaboration with a 122-year-old, family-run steel fabrication business. The collection boasts clean, modern lines with classic detailing. This allows her accent pieces to complement almost any style. I love that fact that Lucy's line is produced in the South, one piece at a time. Her products are fully customizable and attainable, which is a combination that is hard to find for domestic manufacturing. Smith and her team strive to create pieces that don't overpower a space, but that definitely give it some personality.

Lucy Smith Designs was born in the wanderings of her husband's family metal fabrication shop. "I was inspired by all of those steel skeletons and industrial parts. With my creative eye, I realized that the family's old school capabilities combined with modern equipment were a recipe for endless possibilities." This was a perfect outlet for Smith, following a hiatus from interior design to stay home with her youngest daughter. While her daughter napped, Smith kept her creativity flowing by studying furniture and working on concepts. At one point, "I just decided to go for it."

Smith originally saw the designs as one-of-a-kind pieces, specific to an individual client. The brand has grown to have more widespread appeal, but maintains its bespoke origins. Distribution was a big obstacle for Smith to enter the marketplace. She tell me, "Since Alabama is not on the map for furniture manufacturing, it is difficult to find freight carriers to stop in our small town. While planning to show my work at High Point Market, I remember the organizers asking me if I had established distribution channels. I assured them that distribution was no problem. I had no idea what I was getting into!"

Smith says the biggest challenge she faces as her business grows is maintaining a work-life balance. She enjoys being able to make her own schedule, although admits that work issues often follow her home as she juggles the many facets of owning a business. Smith strives to be truly present with the people and things that really matter, but says that some days she's better at it than others.

Smith confesses to some beginner mistakes such as forming some alliances that deep down made her uncomfortable. Those eventually "went South" and she's learned to listen to her gut. Looking back, she says, "I've gained confidence to assure people to seek the best for all parties involved, without making promises that are difficult to keep." As a woman of strong faith, Smith realized that she cannot let these sort of distractions and external factors overshadow what she knows is right and where God is taking her. "Sometimes this can seem counter intuitive to business, but peace holds the highest value for me."

Smith's advice to young entrepreneurs: "Always make decisions from a place of peace. The worst decisions I have made were fear based -- whether it be fear of mistake, the unknown, people's opinions, or losing relevance."

www.lucysmithdesigns.com

# Toma Clark Haines

## THE ANTIQUES DIVA

How could someone that goes by the name "The Antiques Diva" not intrigue you? Toma Clark Haines never intended to start an antiques touring and sourcing company, but as she says, "Opportunity slapped me in the face, and I stepped through the door of serendipity." Her initial idea was to write a series of guidebooks on where to go antiquing in Europe. In order to promote her series, she started writing a blog in 2007 affectionately titled "The Antique Diva." The blog followed her travels as an American living in Europe. She shared antiquing advice mixed with a heavy dose of diva-lifestyle. She wrote about the best places for cocktails or high tea, dinner, hotels and, of course, where to go for vintage fashion. "After all, a girl can't live on antiques alone!" she exclaims.

When the recession hit in 2008, publishers were afraid to invest in a luxury travel shopping guide, so the project stalled. Clark Haines tells me, "I was devastated, but failure turned into opportunity when blog readers started asking me to take them on antique buying tours." After saying no at first as she was focused on writing her series of guidebooks, she later saw the potential for a business when the third potential client asked for a tour. Clark Haines finally agreed, and it immediately changed the course of her business… and her life.

Founded at the height of the global economic recession, The Antiques Diva & Co beat the odds and was listed in *Forbes* magazine as of the 100 businesses that not only survived the recession, but thrived in it. Clark Haines'

company has grown from a one-woman operation into the largest antiques touring and sourcing company in Europe. She now works with 18 locally based sourcing guides and operates her tours in eight countries.

The start of Clark Haines' business included a few naysayers. When her book series wasn't published, people encouraged her to throw in the towel and channel her energy towards what they thought would be a more economically viable business models. "People thought I was crazy when I told them I was going to start a luxury-based service involving both travel and interior design at the height of the recession." Clark Haines trusted her instincts and followed a vision others couldn't understand. She became an overnight success.

Like many of us, one of the biggest challenges Clark Haines has faced as a business owner is not having enough time in the day. "Running a company is a sure-fire way to guarantee that you will be sleep deprived." Clark Haines created a system for organizing her schedule to block time for certain tasks so that she maximizes her energy mode. For example, she finds that lumping all of her administrative tasks together in an hour or so goes much faster than if randomly done throughout the day.

Clark Haines believes the secret to her success lies in her company's ability to be adaptable. Her target market has changed since the start of her company, and she has adapted her service to fit the changing needs of her client base. As she says, "We started out appealing to tourists, but within two years our client base changed to 75 percent trade customers." She now focuses much of her marketing efforts to interior designers, antique dealers, hoteliers and developers. Being adaptable to her changing customer base has helped solidify her place in the market. Clark Haines' future plans include expanding her company across the rest of Europe and into Asia. As she says, "Worldwide Diva Domination!" Watch out!

Clark Haines' advice to young entrepreneurs: "A lot of people talk about starting a company, but the only people that succeed in this business are those who just go for it. Do not wait until you are perfect. Just do it! The more you do it, the better you will become."

www.antiquesdiva.com

218

# Sally Bennett

## MIRTH STUDIO

Sally Bennett and I met through social media. With a simple comment from her, "Hey! We're neighbors!", I became a fast fan of this Charleston-based artist. Mirth Studio was born out of Bennett's need to renovate her James Island, South Carolina home. With years of experience as a decorative painter in New York under her belt, Bennett set out to find decorative flooring for her new home that would survive her 2-year old son. Bennett realized that wood floor tiles could be painted and would be as she says, "much more Mommy friendly." She discovered there was nothing like this available in the marketplace. After months of hard work researching the wood flooring industry, she finally found a manufacturing process that would produce durable wood tiles that would boast her beautiful designs. The tongue and groove design made installation a breeze. As Bennett says, "It didn't take me long to realize that I was sitting on something much bigger than my foyer floor!"

With a portfolio of patterns in hand and a
manufacturer solidified, Mirth Studio emerged right
alongside Bennett's new home. Bennett says, "nearly
every floor in the house is a prototype." Not only
did Bennett find a solution for her own renovation
project, she created a unique niche to fill a void in
the design industry. Her collections are constantly
evolving. Her product line has expanded to wall tiles,
stair risers, wallpaper and dance floors.

Early on, Bennett had to convince her husband
to finance the early stages of development. She
dismissed those who thought it was a big risk to
take. As Bennett says, "Just like any start-up, it took
a lot to gather the momentum necessary for Mirth
Studio to come to fruition." One of Bennett's biggest
challenges has been gaining exposure without a large
marketing budget. "We have to gain attention by
reaching out on our own to create opportunities
to have our product seen by as many people as
possible."

Bennett admits that trying to successfully scale and grow the business has been difficult. There are many components to her product, and sourcing and working with manufacturers can be challenging. Bennett met a successful businessman early on that manufactures wood products. He took her under his wing and showed her the ins and outs of running a successful business. As she says, "From reading the P/L statements to introducing me to trustworthy suppliers, he has been an enormous help and mentor to me."

Bennett's future plans include bringing the production of her products in house through building her own manufacturing facility in the U.S. This will allow her to be a part of every aspect of the production process and to touch and feel the fruits of her labor. As she says, "I'm a maker by nature and I want to continue making-- and making money wouldn't hurt either!"

Thinking of starting your business? Bennett's advice is, "Don't give up! Expect to be broke for awhile with no guarantee that it will pay off. You'll have the occasional terrible day, and your dream will seem dauntingly out of reach. However, those moments when everything falls into place, and you're holding the tangible product in your own hands more than makes up for the hard times." Bennett's favorite quote and daily reminder is, "Happiness is the pursuit of a worthwhile goal."

www.mirthstudio.com

## Acknowledgements

A special thank you to those who worked tirelessly on this project:

**Rachel Mountis**, Head of Business Development for Taylor Burke Home
**Kayla Wall**, PR and Accounts Manager for Taylor Burke Home
**McKenna Madigan**, Marketing and Accounts Manager for Taylor Burke Home
**Gretchen Aubuchon** and **Brendan Von Enck**, Fashion + Decor

# Photography Credits

**Title**
2 One Kings Lane

**Foreword**
Christina Wedge Photography

**Julianne Taylor**
10 Alli Elmunzer of Turquoise & Palm
13 One Kings Lane
14 Alli Elmunzer of Turquoise & Palm
17 Photo Brennan Wesley, Interiors by Krystine Edwards
18 One Kings Lane (top)
Alli Elmunzer of Turquoise & Palm (bottom)
21 Americasmart

**Megg Braff**
22: Erica George Dines; 24, 27: Tria Giovan
25, 26: Josh Gibson

**Ashley Childers**
All images: Rhett Peek

**Jill Sorensen**
28, 30: Tanya Malott; 31: Stacy Zaron Goldberg
33: Geoffrey Hodgdon

**Dana Gibson**
All images: Kip Dawkins

**Emily McCarthy**
All images: Kelli Boyd Photography

**Anna Brockway**
All images: Rus Anson
52: Store - Inside Home, Chicago
57: Store - MIDCENTURYLA, Los Angeles

**Katie Kime**
All images: Kate LeSueur

**Ann Yancy**
66: Interiors by Owens and Davis Design
68: Interiors by Jenny Wolf Interiors
69: Interiors by Amie Corely Interior Design

**Beth Lacefield**
70: Rob Brenson; All others: Brian Bieder

**Lauren Renfrow**
76: Carter Rose Photography
All others: Kauwuane Burton Photography

**Lindsay Cowles**
90 Brantley Photography, Robert and Carmel Brantley
Interiors by Melida Williams Interior Design, Inc.
Melida Williams, ASID
91 Interiors by Stone Textile, Interior Designer Elizabeth Mollen
93 Gordon Gregory, Interiors by Janie Molster Designs,
92 Cynthia Lynn Kim, Interiors by Alexandra Kaehler Design,
88 Matt Licari

**Susan Hornbeak-Ortiz:**
All: James Cassimus

**Mandy Kellogg Rye**
All images: Rustic White

**Victoria Larson**
All images: Lee Kriel Photography

**Jamie Dietrich**
All images: Sean Hogan

**Lynai Jones**
116: Rachel Hanel; All others: Wesley Hall

**Lori Dennis and Kelli Ellis**
All images: Myron Hensel Photography

**Rivers Spencer**
132, 137, 139: Tim Black
134, 136: Sara Essex Bradley

**Cari Cucksey**
All images: Cari Cucksey

**Maggie Mielczarek**
All images: John A. Gessner/Anne Lang

**Stacy Kunstel**
157: John Bessler (interiors by Denise McGaha)
156: Rustic White (tabletop design by Mandy Moore)
152, 155: Michael Partenio
154: Michael J. Lee (interiors by Julianne Covino)

**Mary Catherine Folmar**
160-161: Dustin Peck Photography
(interiors by Lisa Mende Design, styling by Susan Johnson Smith)

**Sherrill Canet**
166, 167: Nick Johnson; 168: Tim Lee; 170: Tria Giovan

**Jill Rosenwald**
All images: Somerby Jones

**Roxy Te Owens**
178: Elizabeth Shrier; 181 top right: Courtney Apple
All others: Roxy Te

**Kat Mulford and Lee Lesley**
184: Eric Lusher
188: Interiors and photography by Catherine M. Austin
All others: Photography and styling by Addison Weeks

**Barbara Cosgrove**
190: Tim Pott; All others: Aaron Leimkuehler

**Beth Collier**
All images - Meredith Loughlin

**ML Littlefield**
202: Matthew Simmonds; 204, 205: Bill Aultman
207: Laurey W. Glenn/Southern Living

**Lucy Smith**
208: Jean Allsopp

**Toma Clark Haines**
219: Lorfords Antiques; 214: Jose Manuel Alorda
217 top left: Jose Manuel Alorda
217 top right: Lorfords Antiques

**Sally Bennett**
220: Cody Deer; All others: Clay Austin

**Back Cover**
Alli Elmunzer of Turquoise & Palm

Book Design by Minh Tran